The Balanced Scorecard

Enhance your performance

through strategic goals

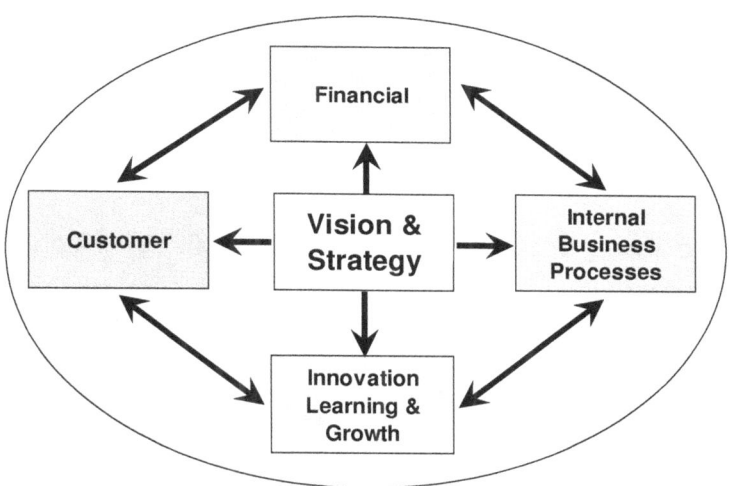

A practical Primer from Alpha Technical Associates, LLC.

Dr. Donald Gusfa Ed.D, Kenneth Gusfa, Daniel Stanley

A note from the author's…..

We at Alpha Technical Associates, LLC are confident the information we share with you will enhance your understanding of the Balanced Scorecard concept. We strive to disseminate complex business, process and quality related information into a simple easy to understand text. We originally founded Alpha Technical Associates, LLC because of our experience with a multitude of Quality Tools, the Lean Process and the Six Sigma methodology. Our associates provide additional expertise in the areas of operation and strategic management, supply chain management, and international business.

Our company founders are International Quality Federation Certified Master Black Belts that began their careers as manufacturing engineers in the automotive industry. Faced with the daily challenges of manufacturing that jeopardize quality, profitability and customer satisfaction, they witnessed first hand, the right way and wrong way to resolve problems. The disciplined methodology of Six Sigma helped them eliminate inefficiencies and defects while implementing permanent corrective actions that saved millions of dollars and increased customer satisfaction. Applying the process and witnessing the results fueled their passion for the Six Sigma methodology.

THE BALANCED SCORECARD

T he *"Balanced Scorecard"*, developed in the early 1990's by Kaplan and Norton, is a <u>strategic planning</u> and <u>management process</u> that uses a balanced set of dimensions, commonly referred to as metrics, to assess, monitor, and drive the vision and/or strategy of a business. It is a <u>process to monitor performance to strategic goals</u>.

Traditionally, companies measured success in profits, the "Bottom-Line". Profitability, in reporting financial statements, was measured exclusively using generally accepted accounting principles (GAAP):

- **Historical cost principle** - for assets and liabilities

- **Revenue recognition principle** - for accrual basis accounting

- **Matching principle** – for expenses and revenue

The Corporate Balance Sheet				
Assets			**Liabilities**	
Current Assets:			**Current Liabilities:**	
Cash	$	100,000	Short Term Debt	$ 60,000
Accounts Receivable	$	80,000	Accounts Payable	$ 100,000
Mechandise Inventory	$	200,000	Salaries	$ 220,000
Total Current Assets	$	380,000	**Total Current Liabilities**	$ 380,000
Plant & Equipment:			Long Term Debt	$ 40,000
Equipment	$	60,000	**Total Liabilities**	$ 420,000
Less: Accumulated Depreciation	$	(4,000)	Owner's Equity	$ 16,000
Total Assets	$	436,000	**Total Liabilities & Owner Equity**	$ 436,000

The process lacked business acumen. It combined the knowledge and understanding of the financial and accounting aspects, but neglected to incorporate the customer, marketing and operational functions of an organization.

The balanced scorecard process is neither an accounting nor an economic pathway to success. Those disciplines, which evolved and prospered for hundreds of years, are sufficient for simple performance management, however, they lack the ability for a business to maximize it's potential. Conventional businesses merely have a goal to make money. Are they actually maximizing profits, minimizing losses and delivering ultimate customer satisfaction? Probably not. So lets explore the balanced scorecard process.

Those who run a business have a responsibility to be moral and ethical. They need to be passionate about the product or service they provide. It is not the business, but the people who own the business. Who wants a reputation for shoddy products or substandard service. Business passion starts with a clearly defined vision. In developing a business plan, determine the ultimate goal. What do you hope to accomplish?

A vision is a statement of <u>long-term goals</u>, whether achievable or not.

Vision (Mission) Statements

- We want to solve world hunger.

- We want to be the most economical clothing retailer.

- We want to manufacture a dependable vacuum cleaner.

- We want to make the best pizza in the world.

Example A

Little Caesars, a national chain Pizza Company's mission statement

"Our mission is to provide delicious, high-quality products at an affordable price, with friendly, prompt, and courteous service."

Example B

The Girl Scouts of America

"Girl Scouting builds girls of courage, confidence, and character, who make the world a better place. "

While a <u>vision</u> states the ultimate path or goal of the organization, a <u>strategy</u> develops the path to follow. How do we solve world hunger without a path to get there? We need a strategy!

A strategy is a plan of action used to achieve the goal.

Let's see the strategy statements associated with the prior vision statements.

Strategy Statements

- Operate a charitable food bank to feed the city's poor using corporate donations.
- Resell year old, chain store clothing inventories at a substantial discount.
- Manufacture the best vacuum design using state-of-the-art equipment.
- Make pizza using the finest and freshest ingredients at a fair price.

Once a business develops both a vision and strategy, they are now ready to work with the business tools of the balanced scorecard. These tools are designed to monitor comprehensive performance. The four basic business tools or perspectives are:

I. Financial

II. Customer

III. Internal Business Processes

IV. Learning, Growth & Innovation

I. Financial

How does your organization measure financial health?

- Determine your Return on Investment (ROI), a GAAP metric.
    - Measures investment profitability.
    - A calculated ratio.
    - A healthy business has an ROI > 1.0
        - Do you want to make $1 for every dollar invested, or would you rather make $2 or $3?

$$\textbf{Return on Investment (ROI)} = \frac{(\text{Gain from Investment} - \text{Cost of Investment})}{\text{Cost of Investment}}$$

An example of a ROI calculation

1. You open a lemonade stand at the local flea market and after one weekend, you determine that you collected $12.50 per gallon of lemonade sold.
2. You calculate your cost for the lemons, cups, and sugar at $3.25 per gallon sold.
3. Your profit is actually $12.50 - $3.25 = $9.25
4. Your ROI = ($12.50 – 3.25) / ($3.25) = 2.85
5. This indicates your ROI is 2.85 times greater than your investment. A very profitable venture.

- Do you deliver Shareholder Valve?

Are the investors of the company receiving a good return on their investment through growth, expansion, shares of stock, dividends, etc?

An example of a shareholder value calculation

You convince five family members to go in with you to open a Dollar Store. You ask them each for $10,000 with the promise of a yearly 5% return, as well as a plan to pay back their initial investment (loan) over the next four years. You use this $50,000 plus your own $10,000 to start the business. You will need to deliver $500 per investor as a 5% return, as well as paying back $1/4^{th}$ of their initial investment at the end of the year.

- **Revenue** = Gross 1st Year Receipts
  = $94,000
- **Expenses** = Building, salaries, utilities, inventory, etc.
  = $37,000
- **Profit** = Revenue – Expenses
  = ($94,000 - $37,000) = $57,000

You give each investor the following after year one.

- $500 Return on their investment (5% of initial Investment)
- $2,500 payback of their initial investment (The Loan)
- ($500 x 5) + ($2,500 x 5) = $15,000 payout to all five investors
- Your take home profit is $42,000

The investors can now decide whether to reinvest the money back into the business to help it grow, or pocket the money.

o **Establish annual budget objectives and a business plan.**
  - Allocate a specific amount of money for utilities, inventory, advertising, training, incidentals, equipment investment, expansion...
  - Reserve enough capital to cover initial start-up expenses.

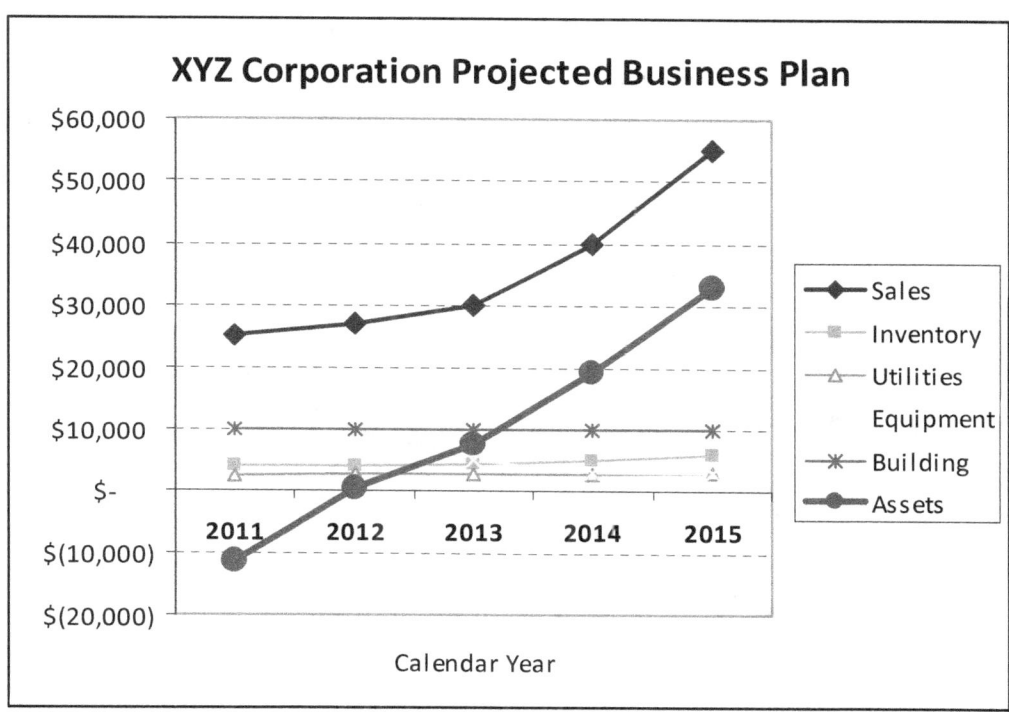

o **Establish a specific percentage of growth target year-over-year.**

  - If you decide you need a 5% growth in sales, year after year, how will you accomplished this? Will you reinvest into the business, explore other products and services to offer, or expand your territory, ect?

II. Customer

How do you use the voice of the customer?

- How do people perceive your company & products?

o Do you offer great value at a good price, or are your products poor in quality and unreliable?
o Is the product or service consistent each time the customer uses it, or do they never know what to expect? (Example: Hot pizza the first time, cold pizza the next time and the wrong toppings on the third visit).
o Does your company name cause consumers to think of the product or service in a negative way?
o Do you achieve customer satisfaction?
  ▪ Do you have repeat business from the same customers?
  ▪ Do people buy your product or service because of recommendations or word of mouth from a friend or family member?
o Do your customers have surprise and delight?
  ▪ Does your product or service have additional features that pleasantly surprise the consumer?
  ▪ Did they get a little more than what they expected?

The voice of the customer can be both internal, as well as external to your business. If you manufacture a product that has to go to another station for processing, then that processing station is your customer. All along the supply chain, one alters, modifies, or processes an item that gets passed along to the next customer. Know who the customer is before you try to solve the big problem.

Some examples of external customer complaints:

- My current customers always complain their pizza is delivered cold or with the wrong toppings.

- The mechanic at the automotive repair shop never seems to fix my vehicle properly the first time.

- The user's manual is so confusing and hard to read; I do not know who to call.

- My patients complain that their appointments are always between 30 and 45 minutes late.

- Every time I buy Brand X, the product always breaks.

Some examples of internal customer complaints:

- We always have to scrap approximately 10% of what we manufacture.

- We never seem to retain employees after we have spent time and money for their training.

- The parts from Station 17 always have burrs on the edge.

- I can never read the supervisor's handwriting on the work instructions.

- I always have to recut the vegetables for the Salad Bar.

- The office manager always orders the wrong supplies.

Get to know and understand the voice of the customer

III. Internal Business Process

What do you do, and are you any good at it?

- What are your performance metrics?
    - How long does it take to produce your product?
    - Is there excess idle time between operations?
    - Are you the first to market with the latest technology?
    - Are you the lowest cost, highest quality producer?

- Are you Best-in-Class (BIC)?
    - Is your company or product the benchmark or gold standard for what you provide?
    - Does your product or service sell based on mere reputation?
    - How do you stack up to the competition?

- Have you minimized scrap and excess inventory?
    - Do you tie up a lot of money in raw materials and finished goods inventory?
    - Do your processes generate excess defects or rework?

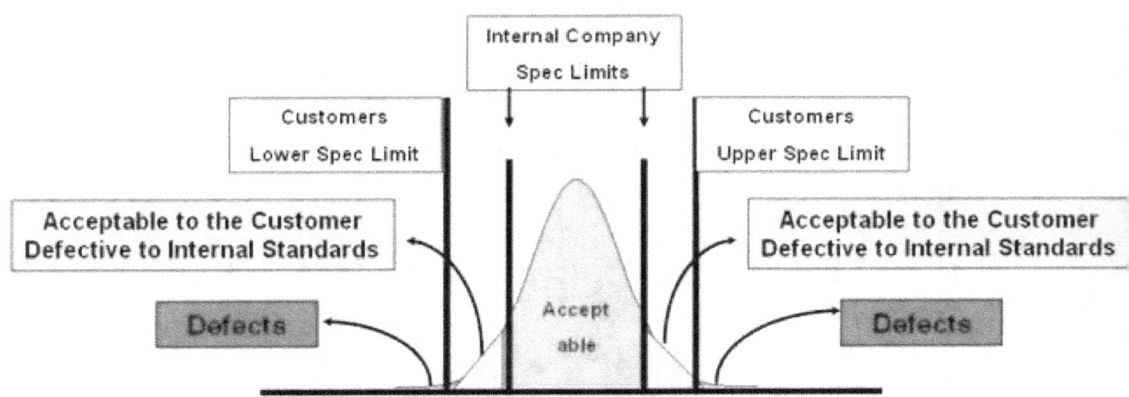

IV. Innovation, Learning and Growth

What does your company do to be innovative, learn new concepts, and grow?

- Are you always looking for new ideas?
- Do you have an active training program for your employees?
- Do you expand operations to meet demand?
- Do you have an employee suggestion program?

The Balanced Scorecard Flow Diagram

Let us see how these four perspectives relate and link to our vision and strategy by looking at a simple example to tie these four perspectives together.

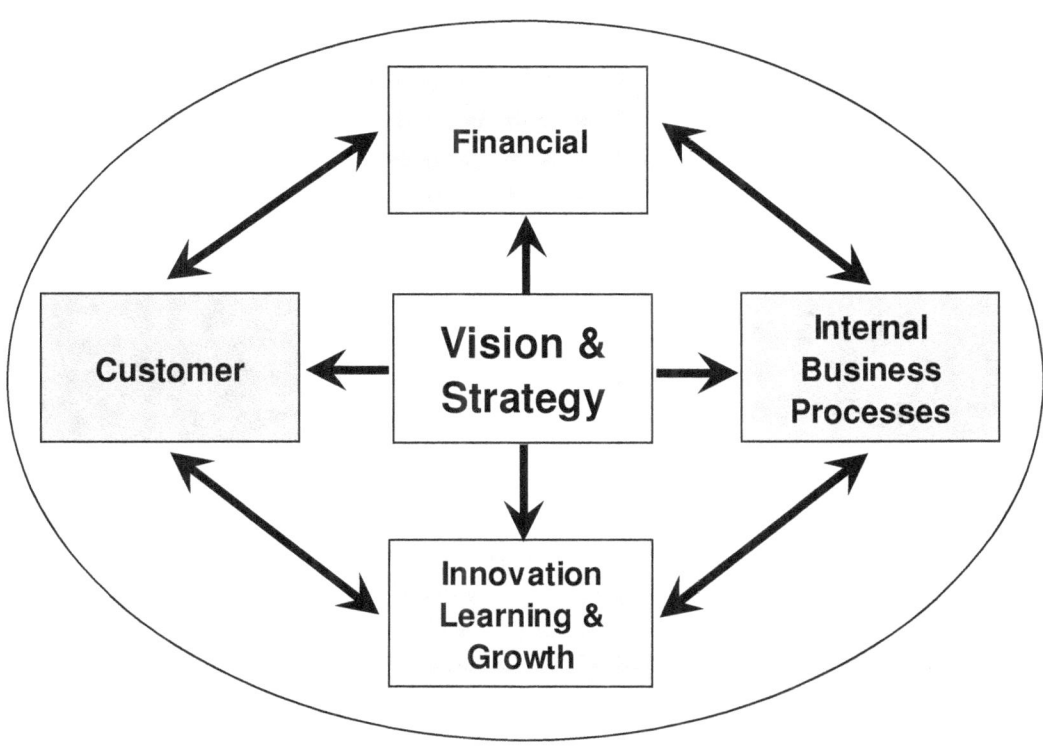

The Italian Restaurant – Example of a changing vision

Your family owns an Italian restaurant, which has been in business for over 40-years. Your grandfather started the business when he migrated here from Italy, and it has been passed down from your father to you, the eldest son. You do not share the same passion (vision) as the rest of the family. Why would you want to run a restaurant anyway, the long hours, the employee problems, sounds like a real hassle? Besides, you have an MBA, and aspirations to do well in the business world; however, you don't care about the restaurant business, it's employees or customers. Your goal is to make a lot of money then sell the business and find something more profitable. In MBA School you learned how to map out a balanced scorecard. Maybe this will help you better understand if the restaurant is achieving maximum profitability. What was your grandfather's goal? What was your father's goal? Isn't the goal in life to make a lot of money?

You decide to talk to your grandfather and father to understand their initial vision and strategy for the restaurant. You then make a list of your vision, and the strategy of the restaurant:

Your Grandfather:

Vision:

- Bring a bit of Italy to America.

Strategy:

- Provide wholesome food of good quality at an affordable price to the Italian immigrants of the community.

Your Father:

Vision:

- Carry on my father's tradition of running the restaurant to provide jobs for my family and maintain financial security.

Strategy:

- Provide good quality Italian food at an affordable price to a changing community, while hiring more relatives to support their own families.

You:

Vision:

- Make a lot of money.

Strategy:

- Maximize profits with minimal involvement running the business.

- Sell the restaurant at a profit and buy a business with better return on investment.

If we apply your vision to the balanced scorecard model diagram, we see that in order to maximize your profits, you may raise prices, serve smaller portions, or use cheaper ingredients. You might hire inexperienced employees at a lower wage to reduce your labor bill, and alter the temperature of the restaurant to save on heating and cooling costs. What you end up doing is degrading the customers' experience in the process. All of this might initially increase your profits, assuming that the customers keep coming back. What are the odds that this will happen? Slim to none. By not properly understanding the balance between the four perspectives of the balanced scorecard, you may lose the restaurant and your plan of having enough capital to start another business.

Businesses are dynamic and ever changing. You need to establish a series of metrics that you can use to assess your status to achieve our vision. You also need to determine if your vision is practical.

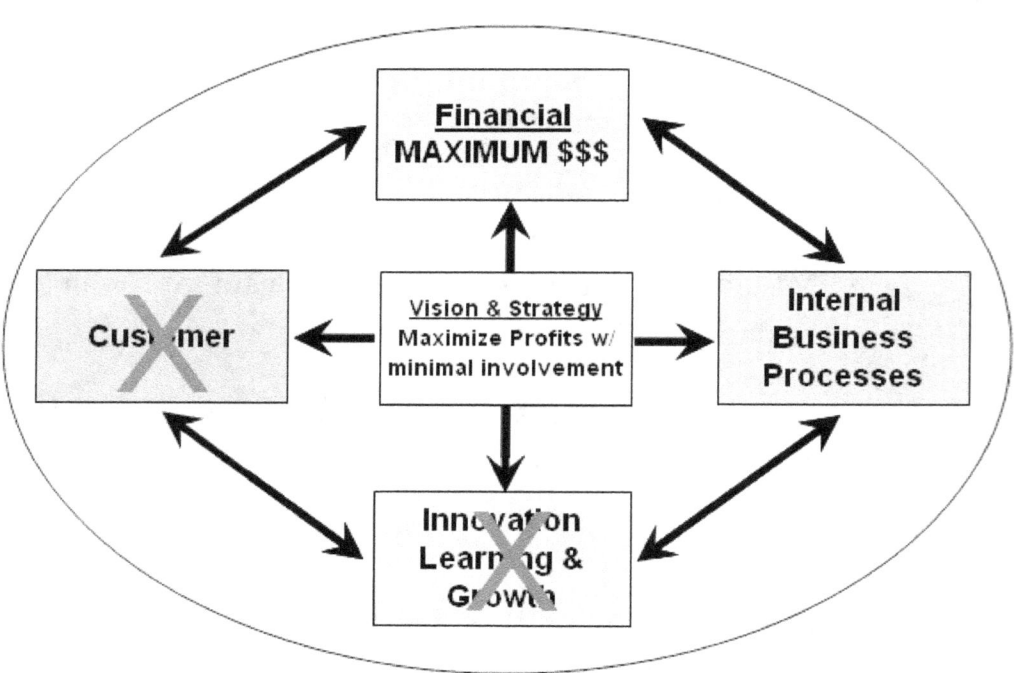

OPERATIONAL MEASURES

For each of the four previous business tools (perspectives), you will need to establish and monitor a set of <u>operational measures</u>.

Each of these measures requires a value that can be monitored and assessed to determine if you are moving toward or away from your goal.

Objectives:

What is the objective?

- Improved sales, additional employee training.

Measurement:

What value due you monitor to determine progress in reaching the objective?

- Number of sales per agent. Training hours per employee.

Targets:

What is the specific value targeted for the individual measure?

- 10% increase in sales, 20 hours of training per quarter, 3% cost reduction.

Initiatives:

Programs set up in order to meet objectives.

- Revised marketing plan, in-house employee training, and instruction.

Let us use the restaurant example to illustrate how the operational measures can be applied to the financial perspective.

Financial

	Objective	Measure	Target	Initiative
"To succeed financially, how should we appear to our shareholders?"	1. Improve cash flow through the business.	Weekly review of expenses and profits.	10% improvement year-over-year.	Inventory control
	2. Decrease energy usage.	Monthly Gas and Electric Bills (kWh & BTU usage)	15% reduction year-over-year.	Controllable thermostat, LED lighting, etc.
	3. Reduce excess inventory.	Cost of excess stock in storage room	Keep only a 2-week supply of non-perishable products.	Weekly inventory of non-perishable products.
	4. Reduce excess customer food tossed away.	Amount and type of food customers don't eat	Balance portions to meet customer expectations	Monitor and adjust what the customers don't eat.

Applying these four <u>operational measurements</u> to each of the four <u>business tools,</u> (perspectives), is a requirement of the balanced scorecard process. It insures that you have a plan to achieve your goal. By committing a plan to paper, you have accountability, and the means to monitor and adjust your progress.

The Banquet Hall

A balanced scorecard – Example A

You are the manager of a regional Banquet Hall. Your facility is associated with a cluster of local churches and fraternal organizations, so it's used mainly for weddings, bridal/baby showers, parties, and funeral luncheons. The facility has one large hall that will accommodate approximately 150 guests, while the smaller hall can accommodate up to 80 guests. Each hall has separate guest entrances as well as a bar/beverage station. Food is prepared in the main kitchen by a contracted caterer; however, you are allowed a select number of other local caterers to provide food. You pride yourself on hosting very elegant venues at a reasonable and competitive price. Your level of income is dependent on both the hall rental fees and the cost of providing food and refreshments for all events.

Your Vision

Our vision is to be the most elegant and professional venue hall provider with emphasis on personal planning for those special milestone occasions.

Your Strategy

- Provide exceptional personal event planning service.
- Maintain and improve the elegant facility & location.
- Provide a professional wait staff.
- Provide a good value at a fair price.
- Exceed the customer's expectations.
- Provide a selection of excellent food.

The next step of the process is to develop the operational measurements for each of the four perspectives:

Financial: To succeed financially, how should we appear to our shareholders?

Objective	Measurement	Target	Initiative
1. Increase net income year after year	Net income	Increase number of bookings by 10 %	Selectively Increase advertising, review expanding the customer base and advertise on social networking. Put positive comments on Facebook page
2. Increase hall bookings to within 3% of maximum capacity.	Number of booking per month.	10% increase for high return bookings	Concentrate on high return bookings • Weddings, bridal showers, Retiement parties
3. Reduce cost and improve services	Food & utility costs per booking	Reduce overall cost by 10% annually	Review alternatives to current suppliers and products for cost saves and quality improvements

Customer: To achieve our vision, how should we appear to our customer?"

Objective	Measurement	Target	Initiative
1. Personal Service	Favorable remarks / feedback	Favorable remarks greater than 90%	Send out questionnaires to all customers to gauge our level of service.
2. Prompt return of messages	Achieve a 95% callback / contact rate	Return all phone calls within 24 hours	Maintain a phone call log
3. Invite all potential customers for a complimentary meal to review our food and service.	How many potential customers accept the meal and book an event	Customers who accept the complimentary meal and book an event (5/quarter).	Invite 20 high prospective customers per quarter for a complimentary meal.

Internal Business Process: To satisfy our shareholders and customers, what business processes must we excel at?

Objective	Measurement	Target	Initiative
1. Take the time to personally plan each event with the customer	Hours spent with each customer and follow up calls	(10) hours for each wedding	Enroll in a time management class
2. Professionally wait staff	Appearance, manners, efficiency	Achieve a rating of 95% or greater	Design standards for all wait staff and grading system
3. Increase repeat or referral business	Track all referrals	(10) referrals or repeat business per year	Follow up with all customers and offer a finder's fee for all booked referrals.

Learning and Growth: To achieve our vision, how will we sustain our ability to change and improve?

Objective	Measurement	Target	Initiative
1. Increase corporate business	Measure new business quarterly	Add 10 additional events this year	Dedicate personnel to solicit corporate customers
2. Understand why customers booked and didn't book an event with us.	Document and classify why the business was gained or lost	Review all lost business and reduce by 10% each quarter.	Follow up with "lost" customers
3. Continuous training for the wait staff to achieve a 5 star hotel level	Measure wait time for food, refreshments and clean up	All food served hot within 15 minutes, wait time for refreshment less than 3 minutes and clean up less than 30 minutes.	Quarterly review with wait staff on continuous improvements

The following example illustrated how a vision and strategy evolved into a deployable plan that is measurable with targets. Keep in mind that you should start by establishing a moderately long list of objectives. Do not limit yourself to merely three or four objectives.

The Tool Shop

A balanced scorecard – Example B

You have taken over a successful family operated tool shop from your Father five years ago. Your Father's customers/business originated from the automotive companies and their suppliers. Over the last few years, with the slow-down of the economy, the lack of funding for new programs from the major automotive companies, buyouts at the automotive companies which resulted in the loss of your network/contacts and global competitiveness, your business has suffered. You and your management team have tried several ideas to increase business, but these new ideas had no lasting effect. You need a plan! You sit down with your team and start to develop a Balanced Scorecard starting with a Vision.

Your Vision

Your vision is to compete in the global market, building high value quality tools, at a competitive price with on-time delivery.

Your Strategy

- Pursue opportunities outside the automotive field and aggressively follow them with our sales staff (i.e. agricultural, electronics, defense contractors, consumer goods etc.).
- Partner with a University(s) in developing new ideas/products, which could lead to manufacturing these products for the market.
- Develop a sales/tooling group in the emerging markets (India, Brazil, Africa, etc.
- Reestablish your network contacts within the automotive field.

- Develop a plan to review your tooling capabilities and decide if you need to purchase specialty/niche equipment or outsource some work to maintain your competitiveness.
- Attend and participate in trade shows.
- Reduce operating cost (equipment, utilities, personnel, etc.).

The next step in the process is to develop the operational measurements for each of the four perspectives:

Financial: To succeed financially, how should we appear to our shareholders?

Objective	Measure	Target	Initiative
1. Develop new income outside of the automotive field	Number of new orders & income each quarter.	Increase "new" business, outside of the automotive field, by 15% within one (1) year.	Assign sales staff to pursue business in areas outside of the automotive field.
2. Increase automotive revenue	Number of new orders & income each quarter.	Increase automotive business by 15% within one (1) year.	Sales staff to Reestablish professional and personal contacts with automotive purchasing and engineering personnel
3. Review cost and services	Return on Investment.	Reduce overall cost by 20%	Review all non-essential cost and outsourcing to reduce cost.

Customer: To achieve our vision, how should we appear to our customers?

Objective	Measure	Target	Initiative
1. Experts at designing, building and delivering high value tooling on time.	Number of bid packages sent from OEM's and completed on time.	Increase the number of bid packages by 30% within one (1) year.	Develop and train new sales technicians to review with purchasing and engineering our corporate strengths.
2. Project and present - or just make cogent presentations at trade shows	Number of contacts made at trade shows and follow up with each quality contact.	Twenty five (25) quality contacts per trade show.	Plan on attending and participating in two (2) trade shows per year (i.e. SME)
3. Project a positive image on the internet	Number of vistors to our web site.	Follow up with every quality contact, with a minimum of twenty (20) per month.	Develop a professional web site highlighting our company's strengths and achievements

Internal Business Process: To satisfy our shareholders and customers, what business processes must we excel at?

Objective	Measure	Target	Initiative
1. Develop a global presence	Number of bid packages sent from **oversees** OEM's and completed on time.	Ten (10) new orders by year end from oversees OEM's.	Develop a sales/tooling group in India, Brazil and Africa to support our customer base.
1. Demonstrate Continuous improvement of equipment and tooling.	Percentage uptime for all tooling and equipment.	Ten (10) percent improvement for all new tooling and equipment.	Develop reliability and maintainability improvements for major tooling/projects.
1. Integrate electronic monitoring equipment with the tooling for improved quality and efficiency.	Number of electronic gages built with tooling/equipment.	Ten (10) % of new equipment will have gauging capabilities.	Partner with gage/electronic companies to monitor tooling/equipment.

Objective	Measure	Target	Initiative
Learning and Growth: To achieve our vision, how will we sustain our ability to change and improve?			
1. Develop state of the art tooling.	Number of collaborated University projects.	Three (3) projects per year.	Partner with a University(s) in developing new ideas, tooling and products.
2. Increase sales and engineering expertise within the company	Number of advanced degrees and/or trade experience	Maintain a 25% advance degree level among professional staff and continuous trade education courses for employees.	Offer tuition reimbursement to all personnel.
3. Cross train personnel in key operations and assignments	Number of personnel being cross trained in the business	Maintain 5% of the personnel being cross trained.	Develop a training plan for key personnel to obtain experience in all areas of the company in order to maintain a high level of expertise.

The following example illustrated how a vision and strategy evolved into a deployable plan that is measurable with targets. Keep in mind that you should start by establishing a moderately long list of objectives. Do not limit yourself to merely three or four objectives.

Robert Kaplan and David Norton are the original authors of "The Balanced Scorecard – Measures that Drive Performance". Published in the Harvard Business Review in January – February 1992, the authors detail the process. This and subsequent articles help to understand the balanced scorecard and develop a strategic management system. The overall process is in the diagram shown below:

Translating Vision and Strategy: Four Perspectives

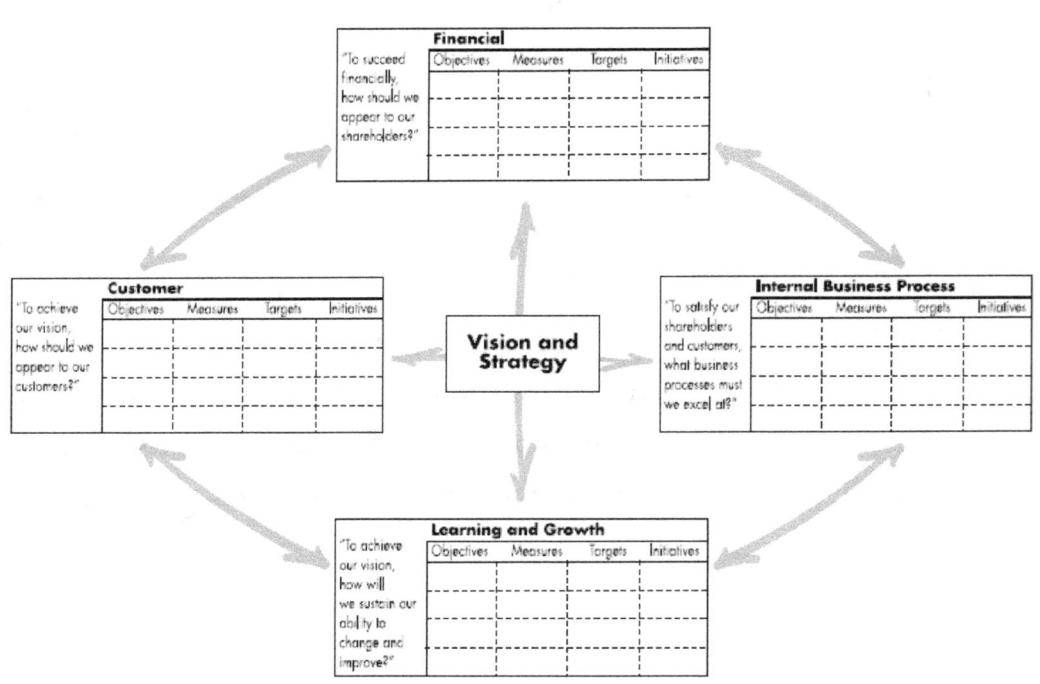

For each of the perspectives there is an overarching principle to help guide your vision and strategy:

Financial - "To succeed financially, how should we appear to our <u>shareholders</u>?"

Customer - "To achieve our vision, how should we appear to our <u>customers</u>?"

Internal Business Process - "To satisfy our <u>shareholders</u> and <u>customers</u>, what business processes must we excel at?"

Learning & Growth - "To achieve our vision, how will we sustain our ability to change and improve?"

The Balanced Score Card can not only be applied to operating a business, but can also be applied to running a department, section, or a project in your company. Review your company's vision and strategy to determine if *your* vision and strategy matches the company vision and strategy.

Reality Check – Lets apply what we have just learned

Your task is to either model an existing business or create a fictitious one to apply your skills at developing a balanced score card.

Overview: Give a brief summary of your business.

_____

_____

_____

_____

_____

_____

_____

_____

_____

_____

Vision: What is the mission or ultimate goal of this business?

_____

_____

_____

_____

_____

_____

Strategy: How will you achieve these goals? What is your roadmap to succeed?

_____

_____

_____

_____

_____

_____

Use the following methodology to create the Operational Measures of the four perspectives for your business:

Financial

"To succeed financially, how should we appear to our shareholders?"

Objective #1 _____
_____

Measurement _____
_____

Target _____
_____

Initiative _____
_____

Objective #2 _____
_____

Measurement _____
_____

Target _____
_____

Initiative _____
_____

Objective #3 _____
_____

Measurement _____
_____

Target _____
_____

Initiative _____
_____

Customer

"To achieve our vision, how should we appear to our customers?"

Objective #1 _____
_____

Measurement _____
_____

Target _____
_____

Initiative _____
_____

Objective #2 _____
_____

Measurement _____
_____

Target _____
_____

Initiative _____
_____

Objective #3 _____
_____

Measurement _____
_____

Target _____
_____

Initiative _____
_____

Internal Business Process

"To satisfy our shareholders and customers, what business processes must we excel at?"

Objective #1 _____
_____

Measurement _____
_____

Target _____
_____

Initiative _____
_____

Objective #2 _____
_____

Measurement _____
_____

Target _____
_____

Initiative _____
_____

Objective #3 _____
_____

Measurement _____
_____

Target _____
_____

Initiative _____
_____

Learning, Growth, Innovation

"To achieve our vision, how will we sustain our ability to change and improve?"

Objective #1 _____

_____

Measurement _____

_____

Target _____

_____

Initiative _____

_____

Objective #2 _____

_____

Measurement _____

_____

Target _____

_____

Initiative _____

_____

Objective #3 _____

_____

Measurement _____

_____

Target _____

_____

Initiative _____

_____

The authors hope you have found this text informative and valuable in improving your understanding of the balanced scorecard methodology. Additional topic resources are available for those who wish to delve deeper into this subject.